THE MAN WHO SHOULD DIE AND OTHER POEMS

(Ocheni Kazeem Oneshojo)

(Palmwine Publishing)

Copyright © Ocheni Kazeem Oneshojo

First published: 2025

All rights reserved. No part of this publication may be reproduced, distributed, or transmitted in any form or by any means, including photocopying, recording, or other electronic or mechanical methods, without the prior written permission of the publisher, except in the case of brief quotations embodied in critical reviews and certain other non-commercial uses permitted by copyright law.

Author- Ocheni Kazeem Oneshojo(Artgenius)

Cover design- AbdulKareem Horlamidhe (creative wizard)

Phone no- +2348119802367

Email: ochenikazeem025@gmail.com

ISBN (Paperback)-978-1-917267-37-3

ISBN (E-Book)-978-1-917267-38-0

Published by Nubian Republic on behalf of Palmwine Publishing Limited Nigeria

Email: info@palmwinepublishing.com

Address- UK: 86-90, Paul Street, London EC2A 4NE

Address-Nigeria: 1A Jos Road Bukuru, Plateau State, Nigeria.

www.palmwinepublishing.com

www.raffiapress.com
www.nuciferaanalysis.com

Reviews

"**The Man Who Should Die**" is a collection of evocative poems by Ocheni Kazeem Oneshojo, one of the co-founders of The League of Young Writers. These poems serve as an imbuement to the issue of sadness and the interconnectedness of sadness and sorrow. This is a good poem to reckon with. I urge all literary poetry readers and non-poetry readers to engage with this work of a prolific writer who uses poetry to express emotions in one of the best way.
—ERINFOLAMI MAYOWA (MAYOR), CO-FOUNDER OF THE LEAGUE OF YOUNG WRITERS

Kazeem has a way with words that reach your soul, aesthetically weaving melancholy and emotive expressions into this collection, which sparkles with images of resilience, loss, realism, and Africanisms.
—Associate editor at Zoetic Press, Durodola-Oloto, Olaore.

"**The Man Who Should Die**" by Ocheni Kazeem
In this poignant and thought-provoking tale, Ocheni Kazeem masterfully weaves a narrative that delves into the complexities of human existence, mortality, and the quest for redemption

Through Kazeem's vivid poems, we are transported into a world of introspection and self-discovery, where the lines between life and death are blurred. The author's use of language is both evocative and economical, conjuring powerful images that linger long after the final page is turned.
—Daniel Christopher (Dan Chris) Author of "THE 25 YEARS PENDING CASE"

Preface

In the silence, I found my voice. In the darkness, I discovered my truth. This collection of poems, "The Man Who Should Die and Other Poems", is a reflection of my inner world – a world of shadows, whispers, and echoes. It's also a good observer of our own world. With theme of loss, love, hope, sorrows and happiness. I use my pen to write them all as a good observer of myself and the world at large.

Through these poems, I invite you to step into my soul, where the boundaries between life and death, love and loss, are blurred. Let us wander together through the labyrinth of human experience, where every step reveals a new fragment of ourselves.

May these poems be a mirror, reflecting your own struggles, hopes, and fears. May they be a whisper, reminding you that you are not alone in your journey.

Thank you for joining me.

— **Ocheni Kazeem Oneshojo**

Acknowledgment

I would like to express my deepest gratitude to the following individuals and organizations whose support, guidance, and encouragement have been instrumental in making this book a reality.

First and foremost, I thank Dr. Sanya for his invaluable guidance and expertise. I also extend my heartfelt appreciation to my family, whose unwavering support and love have been a constant source of inspiration: my mother, my younger brother, my two younger, siblings, my father - the man who should die, and my sister.

To my friends and peers who have supported me throughout my academic and literary journey, I offer my sincerest thanks: Onah Joseph, Isaac ThankGod, Usman Bint, Erinfolami Mayowa, Toluwani, Favour, Joshua Obisesan, Olaore, Adeleke, Dan Chris, John, and Ominyi Andrew. Your encouragement and camaraderie have meant the world to me.

I would also like to acknowledge the support and mentorship provided by my teacher, Uncle Segun, and my proprietor, Daddy Aina. Your guidance and wisdom have been invaluable to me.

To the Night of Discourse and Literary Criticism Club, I extend my deepest gratitude. This club provided me with a platform to find my voice and hone my craft from my first year in university. I am forever grateful for the opportunities and experiences that this club afforded me. I also thank Horlamidhe (the creative wizard) for his beautiful design for the cover.

To my publisher, Palmwine Publishing, and Editor, Outside the Box Editor, particularly Rebecca Collins, I express my gratitude for your professionalism and expertise in bringing this book to life.

Additionally, I thank Dr. Ikechukwu Asika, Dr. Gambo Sani, and Mr. Zeal Adegoke for their encouragement and support. I also appreciate the kind words and commendation from my lecturer, who acknowledged my poetic endeavors.

To the League of Young Writers, co-founded by myself, Erinfolami Mayowa, Toluwani, Favour, Joshua Obisesan, Olaore, Adeleke, Dan Chris, and others, I am honored to be part of this community of talented and passionate writers.

Lastly, to my fans and supporters, known and unknown, I thank you for your enthusiasm and appreciation for my work. Your love and encouragement mean everything to me.

Thank you all for being part of my journey. I am forever grateful.

Sincerely,
Ocheni Kazeem Oneshojo

TABLE OF CONTENT

PG	CONTENT
1 - 2	The Man Who Should Die
3	Bat
4 – 5	Echoes of Loss: The Dark Poet with Death, the Dark Man
6	July 31st, 2013: A Night to Remember
7	Sipho, the God of Lightness
8	Litany of a Castaway Angel
9 – 10	Narrow Dreams in a Narrow House
11	A Silent Widow
12	Earth's Gentle Breath
13	The Whispering Walls

14	Passage of Silence and Thoughts
15	Stars in the Night
16 – 17	The Last Time I Heard My Father Sing a Song
18	The Caged Dove
19	'O Student'
20	Under the Mango Tree
21 – 22	O Blind Man, You Are Not Blind
23	Beyond Twilight
24	A Soul's Odyssey
25	My Wish
26 – 27	Tales of Sorrow
28	A Poet's Invocation

29	Christmas in Full Bloom
30	The Tears of a Widow
31	Ephemeral
32 – 33	Ọja Ọba
34	Bodhi
35	Abuja: One Who Settles Fight
36	The Most Hated Man on Earth
37 - 38	A Smile in Agony
39	Don't: A Poem for All
40	Akudaya
41 – 42	Mother Ibadan's Embrace
43	The Songs of the Widows in My Land

44 – 45	Voices Behind Bars
46 – 47	The Drowning Bird
48	Solace
49	Don't Tell Me the Old Man Is No More
50	Whispers to the Night
51	The Whale Road
52	Roses or Velvet
53	Orpheus Reborn
54	The Ridges Are Dark, Full of Life; Unborn Life
55	The Inspector General of Mosquitoes
56	Let
57	Healing Skies

58	Cupid's Bow
59	African Boys
60	A Poet's Obligation
61	Seeking Mother Breeze
62	The Beautiful Bird
63	Wipe Your Tears, Little Child
64	Who?
65	The Poet's Far Unknown Lover
66	True Beauty
67	Forged Lies
68	Peace or Bloody Batters
69	The Vales and Hills

70	Who Will Bury Me When I Die?
71	Death, the Beautiful Man
72	The Seed of Contentment
73	Peaches
74	Poetic Barrenness
75	Don't Cry for Me
76	The Fight
77 – 78	The Road to Oblivion
79	Virgin Heart
80	The Observer
81	Time and Energy
82	A Symbolic Beginning

83	Apparition of Faith
84 – 85	Fragile Existence
86	The Morning Sleepers
87	Green Is Immortal
88	Poetic Voices
88	Euphemism
89	Onomatopoeia
89	Paradox
89	Irony
90	Apostrophe
90	Inversion
90	Proverb

91	Hyperbole
91	Metonymy
91	Pun
92	Simile
92	Metaphor
92	Imagery
93	Alliteration
94 – 95	The Lost Traveller
96	A River of Life
97	A Mad Man, A Sane Man
98	A Day
99	Death, A Gentleman?

The tumult and the shouting dies;
The captains and the kings depart;
Still stands the ancient sacrifice,
A humble and a contrite heart,
Lord God of hosts, be with us yet,
Lest we forget, lest we forget!

_Lord Rudyard Kipling

The Man Who Should Die
(First published by Outside the Box Poetry Magazine)
(Nominated for 2025 pushcart prize)

I saw my father lying helpless in a four-cornered abode,
Surrounded by shouts of tears.
His soul roamed with an aching heart:
to him, death was the most beautiful escape.

His life was marked by the writhing of his organs,
Plagued by all forms of sickness.
He shouldn't have died, yet he should have died.

He knocked on the windows of Heaven and Hell,
His body dripping with stinking sins and regret.
Fate captured my father
And his days sparkled like stars in the Milky Way–
Glorious yet dark.

His soul ruminated on the rumples of green leaves
And the silent whispers of the beauty river.
His soul regretted his actions;
He shouldn't have died, but he did.

His organs grumbled in distress.
In his days, he took to clattering deadly watery glasses
And pouring addictive poison into his fresh soul.
He befriended an addictive man
Who stole souls,
And his life lost direction.

I stood at the door,
I didn't cry or smile.
My father's days were numbered.

I yearned to see his face once more,
But the pain of destroying the addictive water held me back.
I vowed not to befriend the addictive water
And to die by the shout of his longing legacy

Bat

Not that the bird called bat, with its eerie sound
And fiendish skin, is not fiendish,
But me, sitting with my brother next to my fading father,
Looking at the black bird with its skin haggard and a face rounded like owl eyes, makes it beatific.

The beautiful bird looks like a dove to us.
The aroma of its liver alone is draining.
The oil dripping from its smoked skin is overwhelming.

My father will call me and my younger brother.
We will sit beside our civilian father, and we will smoke the bird in the backyard of our house.
The smoke swirls around everywhere, capturing the fetid breath of our neighbors.

After smoking the beautiful bird,
My father will tear the largest leg for me,
And give my younger brother the shortest leg__
He is the youngest bird among us.

While we are busy eating the beautiful bird,
With my father tearing the bird with his strong teeth,
My younger brother and I will also tear its liver with our weak teeth.
My father will pat us on the head and call us future great men.

While we are busy smoking, eating, and tearing apart our sumptuous meal,
My mother and my female siblings will be inside,
While the men are outside eating bat.

Echoes of Loss: The Dark Poet with Death, the Dark Man

If I sit ruminating on lonely nights and dark days,
My pen will dance, and dark lines will come to mind.

A fresh soul once designated with joy,
Now locks heads with darkness.
The poet is now a deadly dark man,
Dreaded by death himself.

Like a dark demon, I've encountered death
On different occasions.
The beautiful bodies of loved ones,
Taken away by this dark man.

Death, a beautiful being, shows no mercy,
Towards anyone.
I've grappled with the death of loved ones;
I've seen tears dry up in my eyes.

For death is a visitor, not new to me;
I've had a fierce battle – my survival.
I held on to death's jugular,
And stuck my hands in his eyes.
His gaze, an ungodly gaze;
My hinge eyes begging for tears with fear.
Anytime I walk through the valley of death,
He seems blind to me.

Death, the dark man, held on to my neck;
I grappled for survival.
I took an olive tree and gifted it to this dark man;
He paused, wondering if I'm from the realm of the living.

I knew death to be a deadly man, a man of valor.
If death knocks at my door today,

I'll open, and we'll go toe-to-toe.

I'll win or he'll win; if no one wins,
 I'll gift him an olive branch – my breath in this world.

July 31st, 2013: A Night to Remember

All of us would have died in the confluence.
As I stared at the mirror-like view of the confluence,
With different birds gliding and singing on its shore.
The day was dark and void, like the day of creation.
Boot men boomed through the night, cheating sleep from weary eyes.

We were traveling for my grandfather's burial, but it had been long.
The road no longer knew us; we didn't know the road to take.
Men savoring the gentle night sat, taunting sleep,
While guarding directions for travelers on the confluence road.
Their gazes told me of an unwelcoming stare.

A family of seven in a four-legged creation,
Smiles and waves had been distributed in Ibadan.
Eagerness and anxiety awaited us in Kogi.
My family and I sat, wondering our fate on that fateful night.

The smell of the uniform men's short pencils was nauseating.
Brown meat dripped with sweet oil on their table.
Loud music jammed, overlapping each other.
The uniform men had hearts too.
The confluence was their second home.
They told us to turn back; the road was no more.
The uniforms knew their job,
But the long, lonely road did not know its own.
If not for the uniform men, all of us would have died in the confluence.
July 31st, 2013.
A night to remember.

Sipho, the God of Lightness

I thought I can write bold, beautiful lines
And verses until I saw the devil scribbling beautiful lines on my wall.

I thought I can handle the long man
Until I saw an angel with a black sparkling feather
Scribbling verses on my wailing wall.

They were with a long pointed cane painted with red and black.
Their cane was dripping of blue blood
And their body was glowing like a gold
While they scribble on my wall.

Little did I know that, they are the angel of darkness and death.

Little did they know that, I am Sipho
The killer of darkness and the beholder of lightness.
I saw them romancing my wall with their infected ink.

But I grabbed their neck and feathers
And their feathers flapped while their eyes glisten,
And I chant:

You have come to the house of unknown!
You are welcome to the house where you will be forgone.
I cast you away with the voices of my blue blooded brother.

And they grabbed my blue blooded brother
While I heard the eerie whisper of their voice,
They heard the earthly whisper of my whiskering voice.

Their round eyes was sparkling like an ember
Their body filled with scar dripping of black blood
The smile on their face was a facade
The sounds of our fist was fading and booming
Until I took my blue blooded brother
And stain my paper with an invocation to Deus.

Litany of a Castaway Angel

In the beginning, love was found in the Oasis
Of the heart.
Now we tread in the cave of hatred
The haven peace designated with pieces
The way to heaven heavenly blessed
The way to hell, a beautiful view.
And casting away the angel of love
We are now like the thunder and lightning struggling to be king.
Gone are those days when soothing rain fall on mother Earth,
Now is the day where humans treads towards doom day.
But before we await the boom of our doom,
Let's seek Deus and stare at the moon
And pray to the only Deus in any gong of the rounded jailer.

Dreams in a Narrow House

The severe heat was melting our cold skin,
Our hair strands waving and dancing to
The rhythm of the thudding of our legs,
And the cacophony of our frail voice and gigantic machine.
Our breath booming with
The bang of the collision of our restless body,
And the white-legged being with
A red-pale nose talking through his nose,
Arresting and enervating our eyes on the welcoming chair,
Shouting: "Work!" "Work!" "Work!"
The wrinkles and laughter of different faces
In the red-pale-nose man's house,
A house where the dripping of sweat soothes the grumbling concrete floor.

The tick-tock of the clock was our friend,
In our narrow dream in a narrow house,
A beatific road.

And one hot afternoon,
The soothing drops in the sky struggling with one another,
On the walls of the silent and sunny sky,
With the rasp sound of the thunder
And the flash of lightning grappling with the severe sun.
The cacophony of gigantic creation by the red-pale-nose man,
Locking heads with the euphony of
The blowing breeze outside our house of narrow dreams.
A man left!

An old man with grey hair, whom I have often smelled his oldness
And his beautiful grey hair,
Jammed by the creation of the gigantic creation of the white-pale-nose man,
And the thunder roars while the sky wept.
While he lay on the floor, filled with blood gushing from his bloodless

body.
And the dark-skinned man dragged his body
While the floor made the saddest sound I have ever heard.
He had a narrow dream in a narrow house with us.
And I sat down with my eyes red and sad,
Reminiscing the smell of the dead old man,
With a narrow dream in a narrow house with us.

A Silent Widow

I know of a beautiful Widow,
Hidden under the Umbrella of suffering.
Her souls was weeping,
But the two legged beings stole a lot from her
And she seeks help in her budding flowers.

A Widow wailing silently in a dark room.

Earth's Gentle Breath

When the soulful soothing of the rain patters on mother Earth,
Let MOTHER EARTH breathe and smile for us.

The Whispering Walls

The ink can only cry on a white being.
And where the journey in the walls begins
Amidst the deafening ears of the beings,
And valiant verses are veiled
Inside a four-cornered abode.

No one can hear a voice—a voice very bold—
But the wall whispers.
Like the caged bird, she would sing a beautiful song,
Where no one can hear the soul of the speaker in the walls,

Where all heads are bent, sight filled with myriads of black ants,
Stinging the soul in the abode.
But no one can hear this soul.
And still, the wall whispers.

The aesthetics of lines and verses caged in a dark place
While the soul in the room keeps shouting.
And his eyes are tired;
No one can save him.
And still, the wall whispers.

A bard is a prophet, and he knows a day will come
Where the thudding of legs in rectangular shape
Would come and hold this soul's hands.
And with the whispers of the wall unceasing,
The walls would stop whispering.

Passage of Silence and Thoughts

"O passage!" "O passage!"
Are unsettled and unheard.

Who art in Heaven,
Grant us our olive tree and virgin oil,
And relieve us of our aches and boils.
Through the voice in the wind,
Through the sounds in the wind,
Let us enjoy the mature sounds of the breeze.

Hallowed be Thy name,
In this passage, like the aisle of death,
Where our death might be our birth.
And let a living being walk in the passage of silence and thought.
In the passage where the body is left unhurt,
Let us wail our sorrows and hide from the tide of our mind.
Amen!

Stars in the Night

As my eyes saunter around the sad sky,
I see stars stealing the gloominess from the sky.
My eyes twitching, my legs itching,
And my eyes blinking like the eyes of a fresh child.
The moon sits quietly with its rounded belly,
Staring at me while I wander lonely around the world.
The beauty is not in me, but in the pleasure of seeing
 The sky sparkling and the yellowish moon emitting
 Her beautiful rays on mother Earth.
I am not alone, but with a friend who is not a poet.
My loneliness was dragged down by their appearance
While I looked at the sky, designated with clouds of varying grey colors moving slowly toward the Eastern part of the sky.
Still yet, the sky refuses to be sad.
I stand in the middle of the earth, wondering at the beauty of Mother Nature.
I am sad, but with their presence,
Nor do I care about my sadness, but their demure sight.
My friend said, "Kazeem, how I wish I were a poet so that I could write about this."
I went on without thinking and wrote about the stars in the night.

The Last Time I heard My Father Sing a Song

When I was a child, my father was a man.
And he would tell us to remove our movies,
And he would insert a CD containing only music.
The joy that filled his heart while the CD was
Entering the hall of euphony knew no bounds.
And my mother and my siblings always looked at
The rhythm in his heart, soul, and body,
Following the beautiful sounds radiating from the hall of Euphony.

My siblings and I were only children
who wanted to view the punch and kicks of martial artists on our screen.
My father was a music maniac who sought solace in music.
If music were edible, my father would eat music.
If food were more than edible, I would eat it.

While growing up, I started feeling the touch of life.
My life started fading like the cream in an ice cream.
Not that my life was dying, but I was now growing.
Not that I was not strong, but life was stronger.

Our house was filled with different dirty and old albums on our shelves.
Michael Jackson's "Heal the World" was on repeat.
Akon's "O Africa" was always on repeat.
The cool air from the speaker was my dad's sanctuary.

My dad got befriended by a strange man one day.
And this man wasn't pitiful. We stood by my dad.
But this strange man cared not about this lovely soul.
We sang my father his songs, but he died.
We took my father far home to rest.
And in his burial ground, I saw my father sitting on his grave,
Holding a guitar like a tree.
He sat looking at me with the wrinkles of sadness in his eyes.

He sat and sang a beautiful but sad sound.
For me to call him and move closer to touch him.
His body melted, and he went away.
That was the last time I heard my father sing.

The Caged Dove
The radiant Dove dove into the sky with the ominous owls.
And the birds glided and enjoyed the pleasure-filled sky;
their freedom was their peace.
The circular sky was filled with a beautiful breeze and birds of all kinds.
Like the breeze, he glided happily with the ominous owls,
And the scent of petrichor choked his nose as they dived.
He knew not what fate had for him.
He was a Dove among Doves.

While gliding, a sturdy stone struck them.
The owls had been perching on people's houses;
They had barred them from perching on their roofs and houses.
The stone hit the Dove, and blood gushed out from his body,
Staining his white, durable feathers.
And the owls were used to pain, like a stubborn goat.
The Dove smiled and made a pact with the owls.
He was a Dove among Doves.

Four two-legged black beings came
and dragged them away from the sky.
Fear hit the Dove—a fear he had never had before.
The black-uniformed men took the owls and the birds
And caged them in a four-cornered abode.
And the Dove ruminated on his lovely life, now a lonely life.
Inside this cage, there were birds of all kinds:
Vultures, Hens, Peacocks, Parrots.
The cage was decorated with
Callous metals bonding with confinement.
The walls of the cage were a magnificent wall.
The Dove glided and prayed in this callous cage,
but fate had something for him.
The caged Dove grew tired while gliding in the dark,
four-cornered sky.
He later gave up on life,
And he died.

'O student'
(For my student)

Little did you know, son, the hurdles you're jumping,
A way to overcome the race is by gazing and intent listening to me.

Day by day, when I stood spitting out knowledge,
A knowledge I overcame while young,
A knowledge gifted to me by God.

Little did you know, the knowledge is within you;
I speak the language of the wise, and you speak wisely too.

O student, walk through my steps and see the traces I made;
You will never fail!

I quit sleeping, for the journey is too far for someone like us.
The valleys and hills I have climbed—
My sanity depends on my insanity.
You look at me, wondering where I came from.

O student! I am from this same world;
I have always wanted to help the helpless.

Little did you know, I have borne pain and shakes,
And I will eat the cakes.

If you listen to me, even though I am young,
And I listen to you, even though you are old,
I shall take from you; you shall take from me.

The stride of a scholar is the suffering of his soul.
Don't take pride, my student, and heed my advice;
Never will you fail.

Under the Mango Tree

I saw him weep tears of longing,
Under the shade of the mango tree.
People sat, weeping and wailing, crying for
His father has gone home—a place of rest.
His cry mixed with a smile, thinking he will be fine.

I sat beside him, telling him of his choice.
The serenity among us dabbling with confusion.
He wanted to go to know another realm of life.

His mother cried out to the crowd, "I don't want him to go!"
And the crowd shouted back, "Let him go!"
I stood, wondering what is happening.
I started thinking like a madman.

My brother is soaring far away from me.
My father is gone, far to his home.
They took him away in a four-wheeled creation.
And my friend waved at me in the car.

He is now thinking of coming back home.
He saw how life can be unpredictable.
I called him, asking him of his plight.
"Are you good?" I asked.
He told me, "I am doing fine."
The "fine" wobbled in shrieks.
And his mother told him to come back home,
Home to rest.

O Blind Man, You Are Not Blind

O blind man! O blind man!
You know that one's blindness is an eternal gift of life,
Designated with vision enclosed in a different realm of seclusion.
No one knows why the blind man wants to see the beautiful world.
What if the beautiful world, like El Dorado, refuses to see you?
You don't know that seeing this circular ball,
Filled with two and four-legged beings, flapping wings, and running skies,
Might not want you.

The blind man is wedded to a long and lonely log.
O blind man! O blind man!
You wept and cried, thinking you would die in a life of loneliness.
Your vision can see farther than an eagle's sight
At the top of a cliff.
You are not lonely!
The blind man is not lonely!

O blind man! O blind man!
The drop of rain you can hear but can't see,
The tender skin of your family you can't touch.
You will die one day,
But the visionary man will live one day.
You cried about not seeing the beautiful, wailing world.
What if the world doesn't want to see you?
What if your blindness is your sight?

Like a lonely wolf, you ruminate upon your woes.
The blind man thinks he is alone in this world;
The man who is not blind might be blind too.
What if the world you want to see
Is already wailing and waiting to wipe you out?

You want to see the growing green.
What if the growing green and the budding flower

Don't want to see you?
You want to see your family;
What if your family doesn't want to see you?
You want to see the running sky,
And the sky is already dropping snow?

O blind man! O blind man!
Blind man, wake up from your dream of wanting to see this wailing world!
"I want to see this world," your song.
Hold on to your long, lovely friend
And see far more than the falcon in your home,
For you are not a blind man – you are an eagle.
For you know that the some greatest imagination comes from being blind.
Blind man, you are not blind; you are an eagle that owns the shining sky.

Beyond Twilight

Like the sky, her smiles dazzle with light,
A mix of peace and chaos in twilight.
Let us bear the pain of love,
And, like the stars, the sky, beloved.

Amidst rumpled leaves, I saw a leaf green,
Running away from deadly green.
I think of the stars and think of her,
A head I haven't seen in a bar
Of love, precious but still afar.

I will look for it with my senses not far
Tenderly, my older woman is breeding smiles.
But all her smiles are pretended lies.
She is rare among the heads in the world,
The first fruit from Mother's womb to see the world.

An innocent face leaking sorrows,
Clinging to sickness with sorrows.
That's why I pick the tiny gold alone,
A somber poet can't be left alone.

I pick her and want her by my side,
It's just a dream that came like a tide.

A Soul's Odyssey

Once I was married to the verses in the Quran,
Melodies of verses finding their way out of my mouth.
My head filled with unforgettable verses;
Suraatul Kaaf was my favorite friend during my dark days.
I would sit like Zulu and teach the verses to my juniors.
Days are gone, and I am no more!

I was a newborn, cuddling around the sweetness of the Quran.
Those days, I would sing on top of my voice.
Now, I'm drowning in a running river flowing with no end.
I don't know where its current ends.
A boat will take me to its end.

Now, I've traveled far away from the world.
I am black Orpheus, and my legs cry out in fleeing,
My body breaking, and my soul wailing.
The world isn't fair, with glowing flames on the crescent
And glowing flames on the Minaret.
The burning crescent and the burning Minaret
In the river and the storms prevent the world from sailing.

I fell into the River and saw a slender figure
Looking at my somber soul, drowning in this River.
She took my hands and put a book with a candle flame on my chest.
My hair strands stood up, and my eyes couldn't look into hers.
I tried not to follow the boat in the world,
But I had to follow.
This figure breathed air into my lungs,
And I woke up with my soul searching around for this figure.

Sadly, she is an angel and might not be mine!
I will keep looking and aiming.

My Wish

A house full of books, and a garden full of flowers,
Stood a woman with her smile sparkling
Beside the smell of old books and scent of lovely flowers.
And a male and a female kid running,
Calling a beautiful, radiant dove flying around.
Availability of the four cornered man too.

Thousands of wishes will come to mind
In a room filled with people, I have in mind
My grey-haired mother sitting and smiling,
My old friend coming to visit,
My little baby weeping and crying,
My siblings coming to visit,
Families and friends to accomplish my wants.

That's not what I want…

Tales of Sorrow
(First published by where in the world magazine)

Nigeria is waving her hands to tell her tales of sorrows.
Heads are trooping and gathering to talk about tomorrow.
Like the glowing feather of an angel,
Our lions hold tomorrow,
And the cub too also holds tomorrow.

I have ever wondered that no one is promised tomorrow.
The souls of doves are shining among owls.
Our souls growl like the water in a bowl.
The hoe and the earth with the pen are in a tussle.
All Mother Earth's children might crumble.
The race of us is now a shuttle.

The frontline of the war is on the ravenous lion.
Who told us that?
The dregs of blood on the dog,
How can I believe that?
If the cubs can care about the lion,
And the lion trace deadly breeze blowing us,
Will there ever be an El Dorado for us?

A dog can roar like a lion.
A cat can bark like a dog.
A cub can kill an ant and color his body with severity.
A dog can kill a fowl with his own temerity.
It's not only the lion that can bark.
If the cubs, hen, and dog all walk in a track,
The war of pieces might be peace,
And the woman waving her hands can also enjoy peace.

So the lion can't roar
When his cubs are fighting.
The ant can't build
When his armies are bleeding.

Let the pack love one another.
Let the pack lead one another.
Then we can promise ourselves tomorrow.
Then we can live, not to borrow.
Our growling souls would know not sorrow.
All in all, God owns tomorrow.

A Poet's Invocation
(First published by Everscribe Magazine)

O death hold my neck
Let me breathe life
O sorrows confide in me
Let me seek sadness
O muse capture me
Let me see madness
O life strangle me
Let me feel pain
O humans leave me
Let me live in my Abyss
O abyss hide me from these people
And let me dwell in you

Christmas in Full Bloom

Like the sun rising in the dawn,
Our faces dazzle with smiles and laughter.
Like a hungry hyena about to catch its prey,
We rush to celebrate, without a care.

And our legs thudding towards the brown land
Decorated filled with people
Field is our second home.
The cold weather of the Harmattan on Christmas morning,

Beautiful sounds of trees dancing to the rhythm
Of the trees whispering "Merry Christmas!"
And my friends would tell us Christmas food is special
Even the trees, sun, sky, and animals can testify

To the aroma of goat meat and hollow rice
Scenting around the street.
Fresh blood on the floor.
My old friend in Abuja would come to celebrate

With us, and share in the joy and delight.
And though it's annual, Christmas is a blessing in sight.
We find joy in the celebration, despite the pain
And in the end, love and joy shine through.

The Tears of a Widow
(For my mother and all widows)

The black cloth hung around her neck,
The songs and dirges she sang,
With tears rolling down her cheeks like a flowing river.
And her stories – a story of joy and sadness.

Different heads once gathered to cry with her,
And Death, not a new visitor to her again.
Sorrows and sadness are her companions.

The tears of a Widow are a pool of life,
The rising sun a symbolic beginning.

My mother, a widow by fate,
Throughout her whole life,
Saw that the two-legged beings are wicked souls,
But she clung onto the rope of survival.

Five flowers of different beauty, her possession,
The wrinkles on Mother's cheek are glaring,
The sound of her laughter is ringing,
Worrying about her flowers.

If death can welcome the legend,
Death can take her, but not now.
If death can welcome her, Mother,
Death can take her, but not now.

Faithful fate has been fateful to her,
The drop of her tears, a curse,
The smile on her lips, a prayer.

Watch how you treat Widows,
Their life has been marked with beatitude.

Ephemeral

A thousand kids roamed around
the front of my Grandfather's compound
Cries and smile of head everywhere
The sound of the breeze is unheard
The sight and scent of food travelled far
And the heads all seize mother Earth
My Grandfather is a father

> In his own abode
> Where is he?
> What does he want?
> Time tells the truth!

Ojá Òbá,

At Ojá Òbá,
Legs tread with thousands of eyes gazing
At fresh red pepper.
Unrelenting stares at the sight
Of robust yam.
The choking scent of pónmó everywhere,
And people pave, like canoe paddle,
Pave way for its mother.
Shout of "Ekú rò l'ojú ona jare!"
And the body of different people
Rubbing one another.
With echoes of "Aunty, she ni ba mi ra ja ni?"
And unwanted buyers with
Plastic and polythene bags swinging
In the busy air will frown
At the unrelenting holding
Of their hands to purchase
The market women in Ojá Òbá.

A market where plastic fights each other,
The sight of old houses having survived
The longevity of Ibadan, the city of brown roofs.
Ojá Òbá is a market called market of kings.
Who are the kings in this market?
Food: fresh red pepper, robust yams,
Fresh pónmó, rice, beans...
The kings of food dominate this crowded market.

In this busy market in Ìbàdàn,
A thousand murmurs will spread around.
We all see different eyes, beautiful
Like that of a dove.
In these beautiful eyes, there are thieves,
Harlots, looters, and extraterrestrial beings.
And at the hinge corner of the market,

Agbero boys will chatter
on how to share èjá among themselves,
a parcel of weed smoked to be high.

The pitiful sight of old men and women,
Known as Alabaru, begging
For approval to help with carrying
Of one's goods.
And who knows what weight
Of their fate?
The sight of rich, fat women
With glowing golden rings
And earrings on them.

Ojá Òbá is a city of people, not a market.
And I hear, in the night,
The Alale of the market will take over.
And Ojá Òbá cannot sleep herself,
Only for her to be used
By the Alale again.
A night that is supposed to be gentle
Will be crowded again.
Different beings: Akudaya, Abiku,
Aje, Oso, even Egbere
Will be present in the market.

Ojá Òbá, the market of kings and queens,
Cannot know peace until the end of the world.
Ojá Òbá, a market I want you to know.

Bhodi
(First Published by Crossroad review)

In the heart of the WORLD,
To be dead and alive is the most beautiful thing,
For In this world, the dead are the living and the living are dead.

Bhodi* A Buddhist term for awakening.

Abuja: One Who Settles Fight
(Inspired by Abuja River in Anyigba, Kogi state)
(First published by Everscribe Magazine)

The red land was so dry and fertile,
Plant could dry but still flourish,
But you savor their friendship as bitter as a bile.

Two men fought to own your fertility
How wonderful you are as the start in the milky way
Their fight cost them their virility.

Turning their Friendship to hatred against light.
Touching you eases my fears,
But you savor their friendship as bitter as a bile.

Deadly desperate men of deceit found darkness in your light,
And I found solace in you; for you are a welcoming mother,
A productive mother, calm and white like an angel.

Life is fruitful; men shouldn't resolve to fight.
An eye view of you curse not but makes my day.
Resolving their friendship and turning it into light.

You resolve their fight with a flowing sight,
Bless me for your view turn my tears into Joy.
Mother Abuja!
Their fight was resolved. But thank God
He brought you to ease our might.

The Most Hated Man on Earth
Who is the most hated man on earth?
You don't know the noble man of clean nearness
With many brothers from different mothers
Arms unclean, legs unclean, all unclean.

The man who is rampant like a wild fire
With many parts of his body unseen
Everybody wanted to kill him
He is universal, universal and fertile.

The mother earth is filled with
The presence of this man.
Him there, Him here.

The most holy person on earth is unborn
We wail and badly want to kill this man
He is the father of greed, jealousy, hatred, and envy.

Who can kill this man totally?
Religion came with his shining sword,
He is nothing but also love this beautiful man.

Death came with his dangling dagger to strike this man,
But he only cut his liver
Not his heart.
Money came to clean him
But He is also the brother of this man.

Who will tell you more of this man?
The poet's pen.
Listen to your poet.
Our ink is fading.
This man is immortal.
We poets can try our best to tell you about this man
Who is even this man?

A Smile in Agony
(First published by Everscribe Magazine)

I was amazed by the sparkling glee of her smile,
 Incarcerated by her pain and agony, like a tide,
I went and came, happy and merry by the sight of her sparkling smile.

I am like a meteor,
Wading away my sorrows by her sight and interior,
She is so, so strong, looking and keeping the curiosity of my tongue.

My heart opens and whitens with a widening smile,
She is getting stronger,
Can she stay longer?
The wrinkles and pimples on her body tell a story.

A woman in my dream of valor and glory,
Stood I in a joyful moment,
My heart calm as her willingness to live;
Stood I in a sunken state in excitement.

Then I heard a sound sounding so sweet,
 Was it a smile or cry?
Was it a cry or smile?
My heart jogged around in its cave,
 My mind wailing, saying knave.

I can see her longing,
She wanted to cry, but her face looked calm,
I wanted to cry too, but I kept trying,
But my legs held me back to be calm.
I sensed help in her eyes, but there was nothing I could do but cry,
My head rang with different sounds, "She will be fine."

I saw her back waving at me, her mind connecting with me,
I prayed to God and went home, with doubt running in my mind at home.

A poet should friend his pen in times of pain,
He will see what he will gain, I hope she is at peace every time.

Because I might also be in pain, God save her from the pain,
Rest I for a moment without thinking about her in a day.

Don't: A Poem for All
If all could ever crumble,
Don't grumble.
If all could rise like time and tide,
All will be fine.
Don't wail like the wailing willow.
If all is ever grumbling,
Don't think of the circular rope as the best choice.
Someone can hear your cries.

Behold the beautiful mother sky.
He who possesses her can see your tears.
He will see to your smile,
And you will live, not die.
Don't think of taking the greatest gift
Given to you by the perfect one for your cries.
All will be well in a matter of time.

As you are reading this powerful poem,
Sit on a seat and seek His service.
Well, emotion is like flowing water.
Don't let it push you to the depth of the river.
Don't think of brooding;
Think of brooding supernatural smiles.
Joy, happiness, peace, and love
Are all in your arms.
Hold onto those brothers and possess them.
Don't be possessed by the black demon.

You are the architect of your choice and fate.
My fellow humans!

Akudaya
(Akudaya is the Yoruba term for a reincarnated person)

Let my soul fill with pleasure.
I cherish my life as a treasure.
I was pierced by the dagger of fate,
But men themselves call my leaving a bait.
The rasp sound of shovels and cries
Accompanies me to my grave.

AKUDAYA, got killed by fate,
They said I got killed by those who hate...
I will roam around until I live.
Blame me not, for days are still.
I try to tell them I am their son,
But they can't hear me or touch me.
I tried to tell them I am their blood,
But they can't hear me or touch me.

Everywhere my soul goes,
I am chased away like a rat.
Do not blame me for far-off places I will go,
Beyond states, seas, and sources, like a cat.
AKUDAYA's life won't crumble,
AKUDAYA won't mind your grumble.
I am AKUDAYA,
I will continue to roam
Until I find a place to rest.

Mother Ibadan's Embrace
(A poem for the beautiful Ibadan City)

IBADAN, spreading her faded brown feather in the sky,
Nurtured and surrounded by strong and staggered stances.
A mother who is a mother of all cities, owning the sky;
Supported by the altitude of various Oké hills, all vibrant and healthy.

The mother who nurtures me with aging blessedness,
And spreads her brown feather with a dim wretchedness.
At the highest and rustling roof of Láyipo, I stand
Watching the grandeur of the magnificent mother, as I should...

At a glance, I see the beauty of mother Ibadan,
A boundless beauty that surpasses all beauty.
When do I try to take a soul?
I stand naked, like a deadly demon, dreading life,
And a life I cherish, worthless in a while.

My muse, soul, and mind all jam together;
I stick to romancing the circular rope.
Tenderly, I feel a soulful touch on my skin,
The beautiful breeze of proud mother Ibadan, massaging my scaly skin.

And my eyes gaze at a golden peacock,
Spreading a beautiful abode, capturing my aimless thought.
My mind strolls without a destination;
The beautiful peacock becomes my muse – I see my destination.

And slowly, like a snail, I find a new reason
To enjoy her beauty, a boundless beauty that surpasses all.
Anytime I sit, ruminating, contemplating on the Lagos-Ibadan expressway,

And up to challenge, where different legs and heads
Chatter and strut on their way...

Up to Iwo Road, where the sound of "pim pim"
Never gives room for one another.

Then my once madly memories flash
At the beauty of Mother Ibadan,
Then I gaze at the beauty of a large mother,
A boundless beauty that surpasses all beauty.
The beautiful mother Ibadan.

The Song of the Widows in My Land

The widows sit on the scorching ground,
Where crumpled black polythene bags wearily
Their days of joy are gone,
And their faces, etched with long-suffering, reveal their lonely lives

They gather like bees in their hive,
A sight that fills my heart with pity and fear.
My mother, now a widow among them,
Faces an unknown future, shrouded in loneliness.

The widows of my land sing a sorrowful song:
 May death not visit those who dread him?
For death is a wicked man who despises happiness.
He's unfriendly, bringing darkness to our days; days of sadness and unhappiness
Driving hunger and sorrow with his deadly presence.

Our sons' and daughters' futures hang like the body of bat sleeping
dependent on our fragile hopes.
Let us, the widows, wail no more,
But sing a hopeful song – a song of resilience.

Their voices will quiver with a haunting shout
as big men arrive with lofty strides,
Emerging from their four-wheeled houses of pride.

The widows' wails collide with brusque responses
faces once filled with love now twisted in hatred.
Their eyes bore into the souls of the big men,
And they sing their sorrowful song:
May our cries not be in vain,
May our hopes revive, and our futures reign.

Voices Behind Bars

In our bars of ranting rage,
In our bars of ranting age,
Where our home is an enemy,
Where we can't count the numbers of our dark days,
Where the fear of death lurks around every callous corner,
Where pain and agony battle for undeniable dominance.
The freedom we thought we had is now falling and we can do nothing

When will that day come?

Is it the gbam gbam of the uniform man,
Or the gbo gbo of punches on our gate?
Is it the smelly touch of a body befriended by boundless dirt,
Or the sound of tiny soldiers romancing our ear?
Is it the cra cra sound of fearful food forced onto our plate at our gate,
Or the way our unforgettable experiences are forgotten?

The home where pain is a blessed brother,
The home where peace is an enemy,
The home where death, suffering, and agony are the kings.

When will that day come?

All heads gathered from different mothers,
All heads gathered in a human cage.
When we romance the bars,
We are only thinking of one day.

In our bars of ages,
In our home, which is a cage,
We are like walking dead,
Only expecting the black man with a black axe anytime.

Fleshy bones are there in this cage,
Fleshy hope is there in this cage,

Hopeless hope is there in this cage,
Holy hope is there in this cage.

When will that day come?

Some are there only for a sake,
Some for hate,
Some by fate, some for rage. Let our voices be heard in this boundless bar,
And let that day come,
Where we will sing of unfearful freedom.

Drowning Bird

The heat and sparks of the burning crescent
Descended on a dead and drowning bird.

Euphony radiating in a shining crescent,
The young black bird perched on a dead tree with a dry skin.
A voiceless bird breeding eternal life and seeking Renaissance.

Rituals of mankind abusing the tik tok of the rounded jailer,
Spirituality spreading her winds and songs of rituals dying deep down...

Cacophony of the air running from the rounded skin of the hugging the crescent
With souls in different color.

The blowing breeze can't accommodate the bird.
He wanted to feel the soft skin of the crescent,
But there is a burning flame on the crescent.

The bird glided in the breeze but the sky was harsh and
 the cloud was callous with the tide taunting him.

All heads gathered watching the glowing crescent shining of spark,
But the Bird stood on a tree watching the burning crescent.

The bird glided in the sky seeking Renaissance
And the River was flowing with robust Fishes.

The breeze was harsh and callous
With the tide taunting this bird.

He stood watching the burning flame on the crescent
And his wings was flapping where three Road merged in this River.

He was drowning but his wings cam glide.
He kept flapping his wings

The bird can still see the burning flame on the crescent.
He kept flapping restlessly until he was tired,
And he drowned while his soul seeks Renaissance.

"The best form of peace is is solitude." _Ocheni Kazeem Oneshojo

Solace

I imagine waking up in the morning
To the scent of green leaves diverging by
The rays of the sunless sun.
Watching the mountains shining
And gazing at water flowing from the mountain
In a place where the chirrup of birds will be
So musical in my ears—birds of different kinds.
And my hope is unflickered by the presence of drops
of rain cooling the red and dry land,
To help me forgone memories of chatters and batters
in a wailing world.
In this place, like the mind of a soulful person,
The taste of different fruits strolls around in my mouth.
I stroll around, watching the grandeur of all grandeur,
And my hands gently caress this growing green
And not make me a murderer
Who will maul these young and mature fellows?
And in the night,
The shining sky will shine in this place,
With the moon traveling with the stars in the sky.
All elements of Mother Nature accompany me
in the place the slow-minded people call an asylum.
I will stay in this place, dedicating my care
to taking care of these people,
And the flapping of books is my source of bliss.
I want to stand at the terrace of a house
In a place far from humans so I can enjoy,
As the best form of peace is in solitude.

Don't Tell Me the Old Man Is No More

Don't tell me the old man is no more.
Don't tell me the old man is no more.
His white hair will smell of old age,
And his wrinkled face makes him a sage.

The old man will sit on his cross-legged chair,
Ruminating upon days of taking beer.
He will sit like a young child and tell us
A sad story of his people, among us,
We have heads that want no story.

The old man will smile and promise us a story.
The smile on his brown teeth will spark.
What can he do? He is now in the dark.
His shadow will hide, not himself.
His windows creak and shout,
All morning, he loves working.

He will pronounce words to his grandchildren;
They will show the gap between their teeth.
Laughter will capture the heart of the old man.
And he didn't know he would go home.

One day, the old man was on his bed;
Songs of mourning all around the street.
Tears, tears, the kids and the streets.
The old man didn't die but continued his journey.

I look around for the old man,
But all I can hear is: "The dark man took him away."
Delusions filled my thoughts;
Laughter and sadness jammed each other.
My heart leaps up, finding its home.
I am really sad.
Don't tell me the old man is no more.

Whispers to the Night

Looking at the shining sky,
Designated with a myriad of stars sparkling in the dim and shining sky.
The moon sat smiling at me with joy in abundance.
The moon isn't lonely; the stars, too, are sparkling.

Like the dark days and dark waters,
I remembered my broken mirror, which teared me.
But now my cicatrices is healed.
I found out that darker nights,
Accompanied by the yellow moon and stars, are worth gold.

I was in my four-cornered creature before
Rays and sparks radiated through my window,
And my eyes watered at the presence of these gems.
I looked through my window, enlightened, and went for the greatest sight.

A poet should choose his days and be gay.
Sitting and looking for my muse,
A friend told me she made a wish at the sight of these beautiful creatures.

I stood from my seat, looking at the yellow moon;
Thousands, no, millions of wishes journeyed through my aching heart.
And the greens were sleeping while the crickets chirped,
Mortals snored, and a poet stared.

I decided to make one wish;
I made a wish, and it goes thus:
"With the spirit of the shining moon and stars,
Olódùmarè, make my wish come true!"

NOTE: Olódùmarè is the Yoruba name for God

The Whale Road

On this road, the path unwinds before us,
Navigating without fear of dying.
Creatures, Nature, Humans all around us.
All we can do is keep trying.

The good men and the dull men are sanctified,
Where dull heads want to navigate this road.
A lot of heads might be mummified.
Out of the heads on this road, one can see a toad.

Flying creatures flap their wings,
Dying creatures float on this road.
Bountiful creatures leap in abundance.
If you want to navigate, be bold!

Occupants of this road fear it,
And travelers on the road fear too.
Why can't they all be bold?
The whale road doesn't care about anyone.

The whale road is painted blue,
The middle is painted black,
Close to the end, painted red,
And the end, painted white.

The whale road is a beautiful, ranting river.
Life itself is a man with no leader.

Roses or Velvet

Like the sea shells on the river,
Petals of love I give to you,
Drive my insanity to serenity.
Soaring in a white land with this brother,
A man can prevent his peace from
Turning into pieces.

Do you want roses or velvet?
Do you want gold or silver?
Love her tenderly and use her cleverly.
Where I, the Eagle, will soar over
Dales and hills.

The inner dark room might be
Severe and tense,
So creativity begins from one's ability.
Serenity begins from your own tranquility.

Our love is that of Adam and Eve.
Your long, velvet skin,
Your round, dancing face,
Your lovely, smiling stain on the silent
White book.

The lady I love is from another realm.
Our love is that of an infatuated child.
You are my virgin, chaste leaf,
Wanting me to devour you every day.

The sight of your blue-blooded vein, a beautiful one,
When gulps of water enter
And morsels of rice enter,
My thoughts can't reflect
No other muse than yours.

A pen is a beautiful woman - She is my lover.

Orpheus Reborn

On the river shore, he sat, gulping
Strings and rows rhythmic in the ears of the fishes.
The lake danced suspiciously as it flowed.
He sat, singing and weeping,
Two for two, his head bowed down,
Flashing memories of his long-gone verse.

He spat stanzas and verses,
Black beasts, white bears, hybrid beasts, all came,
Staring at this man from nowhere.
Black Orpheus wondered not;
Like rays of the sun, he shone strong with the melody of his voice.
An igneous rock of a man, he was,
A black man from the race of black men,
Who loved black beyond its blackness.

And he said:
"O ye beasts, listen to Orpheus!
O ye humans, listen to Orpheus!
O ye creatures, listen to me!"
Even death listened to him.
All creatures looked in awe at a man
Whose way was more than his existence.

Black Orpheus sat on the rock,
His nose long and pointed like a dam gun.
His blackness radiated like the morning sun.
He didn't want to sleep without creating,
And he inscribed beautiful songs on the fleshy rocks.

The Ridges Are Dark, Full of Life; Unborn Life
(To you, who don't care about the helpless ridges?)

The ridges are full of life; unborn life.
No one can predict the future of the green plant.
All things including plants have life.

Though kind people possess an unpredictable robust life
Who can predict the wicked ones who harm the green plant?
Men will will batter her at night with knife.

The sweat and toil of the farming farmer's life
As sad as a black owl that lost his plant.
All things including plants have life.

The white doves saw an ocean of green life
And they learn to love the growing green plant.
The ridges are dark and full of life; unborn life.
The green plant cries for man is battering his life.
The beautiful ones thought about the growing green plant,
All things including plants have life.

And you ugly people are joking with your life!
You might be trampled upon by the green plant!
The ridges are dark and full of life; unborn life.
All things including plants have life.

The Inspector General of Mosquitoes
(For my mother, and all mothers)

Toiling and enjoying my sweet dreams,
Ho!I saw someone
Echoing and waving gun in the…

I woke from my dream with sounds of tiny soldiers romancing my ear.
No! I shouted from my dream.
Someone stood looking me in awe,
Pondering why she is still awake,
Everybody knows that I live mother sleep.
Considering the figure; she is my mother.
Ta ta ta the sound of my mother's gun waving in the air.
Only for arresting, killing and chasing tiny soldiers away.
Roaming around as dutiful as an inspector.

Generating a sound that eases my ear, wa wa wa.
Every minute in the midnight with her gun,
Not only to kill tiny soldiers but to protect us.
Every time I had nightmares while sleeping
Ranting; my mother will guard us to sleep.
All will be well in order in our two rooms abode.
Low blood pressure but my mother still act like a general.

Order and peace everywhere
For the sake of her precious gems.

Military zone keep off; the soldiers scent the sound of my mother's gun
Only for me to pity my warrior mother
Sending away mother sleep to ease our own sleep.
Quiet and sound sleep for my night
Under the influence of my mother.
I don't know the amount of praise or money
That I can offer my mother
Only for her to stop killing mosquitoes.

Let

Let he who has a father cherish him.
Let she who has a mother cherish her.
Let he who has one of them cherish that parent dear.
Let he who has none cherish his own life, held clear.

Let he who has life cherish his soul.
Let he who has a soul remember, he will reap what he sows.

Let he who cherishes all life be cherished like gold.
And he who cherishes none, let mother hope unfold.

Healing Skies

Stealing the sparkles of the Milky Way,
Like a meteor, my soul loving the grandeur
Of the shining sky.

All the stars glamour at the sight of me,
I stood in the middle of the earth,
A man who is yet to find his home.

I can now see the sparkle of the sky
Saving my soul,
I felt accomplished for my goals.

In the middle of the long circular road
I took to heal myself,
The sky is a glorious one.

Walking anytime of the day, when dawning,
I will ruminate at my stances,
Watching the shining sky.

Cupid's Bow

Cupid doesn't know the right
Place to shoot his arrow with his bow.
Looking and seeing Aphrodite's face
In my brain, I walk around, naked.

"Cupid, why do you strike me?"
My heart ponders and wonders,
Is my little dove noticing me?
I don't know.
Let's look forward to faithful fate.

"Why does she wave at me?"
"Doesn't she know that my heart will flutter?"
"Doesn't she know that she is my desire?"
"Doesn't she know that my heart will require?"

Cupid, arrow, kill me not,
For I am naked, and I pray my Aphrodite
Should wait for me.
Sad enough, she doesn't belong to me!

African Boys

On the running road,
Legs walk and tread heavily at Soka in Ibadan,
Voices chattering,
 Legs thudding with different people.
Like a madman,
I cheat mother sleep and seize mother time tauntingly.

The African boys talk about their experiences,
With each of them sharing their problems unappealingly.
On our way to the white-skinned men with their bellies,
Our life is a life of struggling and craving for light.

In the white-skinned man's company,
We drip unwanted tears,
The white man,
Whom we see as our savior,
Men of painful peace.
The African boys' bodies grunt under the white men's authoritarian symphonies,
The mere touch of machines made by these men weakens our stances.

Our days of ruminating on what the future beholds are too haunting,
The white men shout, "Work! Work! Work!"
And the African boys rain heavy curses on the white men.

Our Mondays to Saturdays are seized by our restlessness,
We hope to be blessed like Holy Mary.
The African boys know not the day their future will spark,
Or the days their day will be darkened.

The African boys hold onto the rope of hopefulness and continue to...
We work for the white men willingly,
Fateful faith makes us that way.
In our own land, we get paid what we ought to be paying the white and bellied men.

A Poet's Obligation

In the naughty night, I stay vigilant,
Upon the hours I need to enjoy mother sleep.
My eyes and body agile like that of a militant.

Clean water's cooling company is all I need to sip
In my dark and dreadful days.
I am sacrificing myself for the world.
I know there will be more days.

Who will cleanse this beautiful and ugly world?
The black demon will dance during his days.
Faithful fate or failure will find her people.

Poets are the best, beautiful creatures;
We write with stains on our white to cleanse
The stains of powerless people.

Well! Our second home is Mother Nature,
Where we will enjoy her peace.
We will write not to please but to ease.

Seeking Mother Breeze

Now stands mature Mother Nature in bliss,
Where trees wave their hands in glee,
Where showers of beautiful breeze increase.
Mother Nature is also a tree,
Where the unseen breeze spreads her seeds.
All creatures seem to enjoy her blessings,
Gentle and calm like the smiles of kids.
As silent company is all my craving,
Then of her beauty, I must seek.
Mother Breeze is everywhere in the world;
If not for her, whom do I seek?
In a world full of embers, my body welcomes
The beautiful Mother Breeze.
Never! My body can't do without loving
Mother Breeze.

The Beautiful Bird

From the eyes of the finest creature,
Where his presence a man might die,
The fairest and noblest of all creatures.

His eyes round and red like that of an ember.
His presence always leads to continuous cry,
The harbinger of deadly darkness,
Casting goodness away is all he could try.

His sorrowful song, too melodious in darkness,
A sacred, sadder creature clothed in beatitude,
His presence will incense sleeping soothsayers,
Perching on tree branches in altitude
And savoring the gentle night with mournful, prayerful songs.

Pity the world or pity your brothers,
For I fear your presence too deadly
To your brothers.

Your Tears, Little Child

Wipe your tears, little child!
You strive and build your sandcastle.
You are a free child.

Wipe your tears, little child!
You strive to build your sandcastle.
You are a free child.

On the river shore, you dance,
Eating and building weak sandcastles.
The castle is a magnificent stance;
Your worries are like faded memories.

You are bound to enjoy the honey of life.
I remember being you in my memories.

Wipe your tears, for there is enough time.
Don't be angry at Mother Breeze for breaking your castle;
She is only telling you that you have little time.
She is telling you about how life can be funny.

Wipe your tears, for you are beautiful, bonny

Who?

So it is not that the world is littered with perfection
Of the sins and goodness of man.
Where some people hold perfection
And some believe and value sins like gold.

Who will help the son of a man?
When will all the stories be told?
Where do you think you will go?
Who do you think will save you?
Where is even your goal?

Sins are sweet and soulful to seek;
Righteousness is ugly and is an object of mockery.
Let us walk on the road full of beautiful ink,
But wailing in it will draw you backward.

The Poet's Far Unknown Lover

When most I blink, it's you I see,
Stealing my own blood and tearing my heart.
Cupid is wicked and chooses to shoot at me.

My heart is battered and buried in your heart.
No matter how I try to write,
Your faithful figure flashes through my eyes like old memories.

Yours are always the letters in my shallow sight;
My shallow sight can see as an eagle's eye.
Brother Pen accompanies me to write you letters,
So solitude might make me mad and calm!

My dirty heart is full of foul litter.
The thought of you is a wealth that keeps me calm.
In the river of love, I will drive slowly,
But I hope you don't see me lowly.

True Beauty

But where will I stand amidst
Human sounds of searching souls?
But naked beauty in a woman is like a beast,
Sitting and waiting to shine amidst
Hundreds of women.
Minutes and hours sitting down.

Beauty is the companion of all women.
Who told you that beauty is about sitting down?
With hands twisting and dressing the hair?
Beauty lies in the inner heart,
Not only by the spark of your shining hour.

As beautiful as Aphrodite with a shining heart,
With a good heart will you be the most holy.
With shiny hair and a bad heart, the most ugly.

Forged Lies

"Lust is full of forged lies," Shakespeare said that.
"Where the most beautiful lust lies, Lust is full of deception," told you I that.

Lust is like a day,
Dawning and going again.
"Lust can be compared to love," that's what they say.

When humans—servants of lust—smile again,
Lust and love are not brothers!
Who told you that lies and lustful excess desire?
Can make you love another?

Your excess desire will make you retire.
You will be trapped in the heart of lust;
If you aren't careful, you will be lost.

Peace or Bloody Batters

Of what treasure will batters be stolen?
Of what measure will peace be present in our lives?

With no peace, we will be battered, shattered, and broken.
The hands of banging ease their way into people's lives.
The smell of bloody battered people
Touching and eating the lives of innocent folks,
The beautiful brothers who consume the lives of many.

Peace, as fragile and precious as a yolk.
Mortals should seek peace in place of painful pieces.
Seek peace all through my life,
Having seen sorrowful souls battered into pieces.
Their lives being consumed by robbers of life.

I see that peace is a welcoming mother.

The Vales and Hills

I am no longer grieved at the stings of life.
I am no longer weak as a fragile heart.
I am no longer concerned about the vales and hills of life.

Where do you think my heart resides?
Where do you think I run to for peace?

The current of life will flow to all sides—
North, West, East, South, and to all men.
The only being that can free me from its tide
Is nothing but the count of my breath up to ten.

I run for peace, and my heart resides in holy hope.
As long as I am alive,
Never will I think of life's stings or its circular rope!

Solely seek I the service of hopefulness.
I will forever live with my heart full of hopefulness.

Who Will Bury Me When I Die?

Who will bury me when I die?
But my lines and verses are up and down,
Though I don't know my place when I die.
But accompany me with my lines in case I drown.
My lines are a raging fire.
And in later decades, your children will try
Loving my lovely lines till they tire,
So should I see beauty in writing; it is all I can try.
The age to come will think about this poet,
Merrily reading my lines until they know
Where the real me resides as a poet.
My sons and daughters all will know.
But if my tomb is disturbed,
I fear my soul shall be perturbed.

Death, the Merciful Man

In a ragged cloth, I saw a madman
Who sings happily and is free of his woes.
Nothing he knows, but he is a man,
With dirt, blood, and haggard sores all on his toes.
He doesn't know whether he will be fine.
He thinks not about the pleasures of life
Nor the stings that shine.
He will continue to roam all his life
Until mortal fate arches his aching heart.
The road of sanity is a dark life.
His life is caged in his own heart.
Who will change the suffering of his life?
This man called death will take him to rest,
Where the man will rest well, the best.

The Seed of Contentment

Be content with whatever you possess.
Without life, you are nothing but a dead ant.
Contentment is very rare to possess.
When all are losing, do not pant.
Where will you bury your running regret?
Your spirit is the closest to a burning realm.
Even if your pocket is leaking, contentment should you beget?
Greediness will shatter you and drag you to a regretful realm.
Degradation will all that reflect
In your lonely life full of litter.
Because chubby contentment will make you regret;
The truth is always bitter.
I am telling you the bitter but sweet truth:
My son, contentment should you soothe.

Peaches

I sat looking at different beautiful plants.
I packed all peaches in plenitude with a picture painted in my mind.
I took the peaches at my front; peaches of different kinds.
I took the fresh and firm peach out of the four peaches.
All of them are beautiful except one of them.
I am an ugly being designated with deadly stitches,
Intoxicated by the sweetness of my journey like hemp.
I took the beautiful ones and left the ugly ones.
The ugly peach cried out for help.
The beautiful peaches smiled, and they seemed to be the lucky ones.
I buried the beautiful peaches and cried for help,
While the ugly ones bloomed with blessedness.
The beautiful peaches befriended wretchedness.

Poetic Barrenness

Why is my stanza so barren of new child?
So far from falling fateful, feeble fathers
Of madness struggling to birth their child?
Lines, verses, stanzas are our brothers.
How can I scribble when my head is full and barren?
It makes me sad as a fresh widow.
Certain things might make us barren,
Looking for my muse but finding none through my window.
O who knows what we are facing in our realm
And calling careful critics to look into our restlessness?
A poet's world is like a dark realm
Where I will see to my not being barren.
I will try my best, but sometimes I have to be barren.

Don't Cry for Me

No longer cry for when I am dead,
Then you shall hear how my soul strolls.
Why will I ever be surprised when I am dead?
In this vile world, will you read my scrolls?
If you read my lines, remember me—
That leave I will leave with my grave cold.
If you leave my lines and let them be,
Your ways might be lighted by cold.
"O death, the merciful one."
When I am now fulfilled in partially cleaning the world,
Like love and lust locking horns, will you be one?
Do not leave this wailing word without loving my word.
I will create beautiful verses that will never die;
I will make my lines immortal; I won't die.

The Fight

My journey in the forest of peace—
White leaves are what I love the most.
Where I saw two dogs fighting for peace.
Know I, peace is the uttermost.
The two dogs fought and fought in the beautiful forest,
And I told them to stop the gbas gbos.
Where will I reside?
A dark forest or a light forest?
I took a coin and flipped it with a terrible toss,
And the two dogs—white and black—waiting for their fate.
Seek I pleasure in a quiet place;
I don't like the firm grip of hands, not hate.
I settled the dogs by giving them a four cornered lorry.

The Road to Oblivion
(To all the departed souls of Federal University Lokoja, 18/02/2025)

The screeching of the tires I saw
The wringing of their organs I heard
The wailing and crying faces I saw
The whispers of death I heard
The road to oblivion is beatific
The road to oblivion is ugly
Not that I was there but I was there
I Know that
Every soul must taste death.

Skin torn like that of crushed goat
Bones broken, Souls broken
Their shuttle broken and crushed.
We the onlookers must taste death,
Only the way we taste the dark man might be different.

That day's flag was color red and
That day even the road wasn't thirsty of blood.

The colorful cloth of wailing bodies
The cacophony of that day was the salty water dripping from our eyes
Their souls departed from the world.
Hundreds of faces and gazes gathered around,
Every soul must taste death.

What will be the fate of their parents?
What will be the fate of their friends?
The road to academic excellence now the road to oblivion

I was at home seeing the tumultuous atmosphere at the road
The screen of four cornered creation of man filled
With dark text and emoji's
All of us are here in the circular ball
But we can't escape the road to oblivion

The wailing young souls are gone

A poet is penning down his prayers
May their silent, sad, secluded and strong soul rest in peace.

Virgin Heart

Coming to kiss her lips, such grace I found.
Me, a weaning child, sucking breast from his mother,
Petals of her love; a dream I found.
A secret cage in my heart, for she is my lover.
Her face did tell that love is getting lost.
Her smile did smell like glowing skin.
Her lovely eyes drive the genius of art lost.
Her tiny, radiant hands taunt my skin,
A rare breed of human with a virgin heart,
Disguising a weak heart with an odorous smell.
Soon after, my sorrow sings of her holy heart.
My face beams like a victim of a pleasant smell.
    Love, not hatred, is the man of essence.
    But thy love is all I want, in essence.

The Observer

One bird dives alone in the sky.
Two birds perch on a tree and watch him fly.
Three birds hop to a grain, saw it's almost dry.
Four mockingbirds sing, watching the sky.
Five birds saw a fly.
Six birds sing, but they are shy.
All birds enjoying their time.

One man watching from afar,
He took his pen and wrote about their play.

Time and Energy

It took two hours to tell the time, and the tool Tolu used to taunt Titi's tall cat, Tanny.

It took four hours to fall on the bed on the faded floor; Fanny, Tanny's friend, Fanny, flooded with faeces.

It took six hours to sweep the six rooms in the sixth block on the sixth day of September.

It took eight hours to hate eighty-eight people and eighty-eight animals for no sake.

It took ten hours to tell the tale of this timely ten hours.

A Symbolic Beginning

Cheers to life when the baby gets out of its haven,
A place with a soft, fleshy wall,
Rounded like and glowing like a fresh doughnut,
Frying in the pot.
Sweet, sharp melody of cries,
And the stares and gazes at this young being.
All heads will gather, saying to him: "Cheers to life."
But the baby will be wrapped around in cloth,
Filled with cloth made of fitting wool,
Inside the four-cornered room filled with the scent of blood and colostrum.
We still see the baby fondled by its mother.
We tell him: "Cheers to life."
But now the world smiles at this fleshy being
With a loud: "Ha ha ha."
The world, her inhabitants, hitchhikers,
Waiting for the gong of a bell,
All to escape from the wrinkling laughter of the world.
Now this fleshy being, smiling and crying,
His cry a symbolic beginning of life.
The world is a stage.
We tell him again: "Big boy, welcome to the world."

Apparition of Faith

A Poet's apparition,
I strolled like a holy man.
I am holy, but the world said I am unholy.
I saw a woman trekking to the Mosque with her child,
And he said, "Mommy, what about Lateef?"
"He is going to pray too."
I was going to the house...
I stood, looking at them, and the apparition
Of the world daunted on me.
The world is holy.

Fragile Existence

Beware woman,
Beware man,
We are mortals,
For we can live and die anytime.

Bringing life to mother earth,
Like her stones,
Dumping and dusting dungs for her surface.

Beware man,
Beware woman,
We are mortals.
Four hands, four legs,
Sprout life into unborn yolks.

The time will come like a meteor and fade away,
Memories will come and fade away like the fog in the morning.
Sadness will be woven into joy,
Joy woven into sadness.

Thinking your thoughts into something thoughtful,
The crown will also come,
The pen will also come.
Honey will be free,
Life will be free.

Be careful in this spherical room,
We are MORTALS.
Be careful of your desire,
And what you acquire.
Be watchful of your words,
And don't be lost with words.
Don't desire too much,
Don't retire too much.
What you desire incessantly

Might lead to your downfall pleasantly.

Beware man,
Beware woman,
We are mortals.

The Morning Sleepers

In the morning, they see
Like the eye of an eagle,
They view the world differently,
Loving the striking beauty of Mother Nature
With their energetic hands.

Sleeping with the cloth of suffering
Beneath the richness of life
That belongs to them,
Depriving themselves of their lovely life.

Stand up, stand up!
Water drooling from their mouth,
Is the water to enlighten their soul?
They view the world partially,
Loving the striking beauty of Mother Nature
With their energetic hands.

They are making the wrong choice,
They are the walking dead,
As stupid as chidodo,
The bird who eats from feces but detests feces.

I wonder what their gain is,
Dying in the wrong way.
Been in haste in the evening,
They are late.

They should get back to their senses,
So that it won't be late.

Green Is Immortal

My mind jingles
Like a Catholic bell,
Filling myself with perturbed praise,
Not knowing my rightful place.

My father doesn't have an oil company,
My mother doesn't have a stock store company,
My grandfather is a lover of green,
Only from the green I came to being.

Green is immortal,
I don't need to be rich,
Nor do I need to be poor,
With the help of green,
My forefathers and families live.

I will go back to green,
And not desert the ink,
I will feed the world in a blink,
I will do what you will see.

Poetic Voices: A Celebration of Literary Devices

I am **PERSONIFICATION**

P- Popular like Jesus in poetry,
E- Every poet can't do without me.
R- Rarely leaving me and using me popularly
S- "She is the brother of hope"
O- O! Check the last line before this line because
N- Not only am I giving nonliving things attributes of living things.
I- I always respect nonliving things.
F- FEAR ME!
I- I am very radiant like the morning sun.
C- Causing deeper respect between poet and people.
A- All of you should know me.
T- Take not from a brother
I- Instead use me in a sensible way.
O- Oh! They call poems filled with me personified poem
N- Now you know me.

I am **EUPHEMISM**

E- Eulogize me from always saving you and protecting poets
U- Under my protective umbrella.
P- People use me to say unpleasant things in a pleasant way.
H- Hear me out
M- "Man of the people kicked the bucket"
I- In the line before this line
S- See how I say unpleasant things in a pleasant way.
M- My name is Euphemism!

I am **ONOMATOPOEIA**

O- Oh people hear me!
N- Not only alliteration is a close friends of sound,
O- Other figures of speech are there which I
M- Make the list of one of them.
A- "Argh arrgh" that's the sound of groaning.
T- Telling you how i use sound to create images
O- Officer ONOMATOPOEIA of figures of speech
P- Please don't kill me arrgh! arggh! arrgh!
O- Only check the last before this line.
E- Every sound of me tells you more about something.
I- I might sound meaningless
A- All in all my brothers; the poet knows I speak well and they use me.

I am **PARADOX**

P- Paradoxically I might look meaningless and absurd.
A- "All great truth begins as blasphemies."
R- Read out the sentence to yourself
A- As you can see it looks meaningless, right?
D- Dive deeper into it and you will see the meaning.
O- Only for you to know that all truth really begin as blasphemies
X- Xenas of Literature.

I am **IRONY**

I- I always say the opposite of what you want to say.
R- "Read because school is a scam"
O- Only letting you know that you should read.
N- Not only do I save you from trouble,
Y- You should also save me as make use of me.

I am **APOSTROPHE**

A- Always use me to address someone or something that is not present.
P- Pal of abstract noun.
O- "O death; where is thy sting?"
S- See how I call death who is not present with me.
T- Telling other people that I call things that are not present with me.
O- "O grave, where is thy sting?"
R- Ranting and calling death and grave.
H- Hear me out because I am always emotional.
E- Everybody that don't know me now know me.

I am **INVERSION**

I- I am a departure of normal sentence order.
N- Not only departure, but to emphasize words.
V- Vineyard of disorder.
E- Everybody don't really know me.
R- Relaying a message in disorderly but serious way.
S- See for yourself.
I- "I saw ten thousand at a glance"
O- Oh that's wrong; "Ten thousand saw I at glance" is the correct one
N- Now you know me.

I am **PROVERB**

P- Proving to them that I am short and I express truth
R- Read me often.
O- Only I is one of the oldest figure of speech.
V- Versatility is my nature.
E- "Every short man can still see heaven"
R- Read the line before this line over again
B- Basically, I express truth in short words.

I am **HYPERBOLE**

H- Hearing only the sound of my name
Y- You should that I am the father exaggeration
P- Present always in Literature and oral form
E- Enticing laughter is my job.
R- "Read to the extent of chasing away hungers" I am
B- Bold enough to be in a sentence without fear.
O- Oh! You think I am not really necessary?
L- Let me tell you humans,
E- Everybody need me because I am hyperbole.

I am **METONYMY**

M- Man's pen is mightier than his sword.
E- Everybody don't really make use of me.
T- "The sword men came out to welcome Caesar". I
O- Occupy a lot of space with just a word.
N- Now you know that the city in the sentence talks about soldiers
Y- You should try and learn about me, please!
M- Man's pen means education and his sword war or soldiers
Y- You should now understand me.

I am **PUN**

P- Play and play me with meanings
U- Until I am meaningful
N- No one should refer to me as pun.

I am **SIMILE**

S- Smiling strongly in comparison.
I- I am the owner of as or like.
M- Many poet can't do without me.
I- I am the brother of metaphor.
L- Letting you know the full comparison of two words
E- Every poet should never desist from me.

I am **METAPHOR**

M- Man of complexity
E- Every work of Literature use me
T- Talking of complexities
A- All makes me metaphoric
P- Play not with me
H- Heavily loaded with deeper meanings
O- Of grandeur
R- Rely on me and panic not

I am **IMAGERY**

I- International father of images
M- Much of me is needed in literature
A- Always present in literature like a weather
G- Good you picture me while reading
E- Excluding lazy people
R- Ranting on me for my simplicity
Y- You should know that I am a simple man.

I am **ALLITERATION**

A- Acquiring the repetition of consonants sounds
L- Loving me lest don't hate me
L- Learn from the sound I produce
I- Instead check the repeated consonants in a sentence
T- Tell them I am really a close friend of rhythm
E- Enjoy every entity of me.
R- Repeated; red man on a red bed
A- After this line check line eight.
T- Telling and telling you repeatedly
I- I am the repetition of consonants sounds
O- Occupying any position in the world of Literature.
N- Now you know me.

Chorus
(All)

We are the figures of speech
We guess you now know us
Learn and make use of us
We are the poet brothers
We will always make your poems beautiful
We hope you know us now?

The Lost Traveller

The traveler set forth at dawn.
With his bags, books, and pen on his body,
The traveler never knows when the day will dawn.
 He is a mindful body.

The traveler set forth and proceeded on his journey.
He stood ruffled and calm.
He stood thinking about the course of his journey.
He is an insane person who is calm.

The traveler makes friends with his mind.
But the path to follow is filled with doubt.
The T-junction he stood at jogs around his heart.
His mind and soul are in a bout.

The traveler proceeded on his journey to a land decorated with thorns of flowers.
He thought, "Sometimes a journey is filled with honey." He wobbled while walking for worthy hours.

The traveler is filled with rage.
He walks tirelessly like a madman.
He knows not the days nor his age.
He is as focused as a noble man.

The traveler stood and looked again,
 With four heads looking at his stance.
The four heads say he is mad again.
 He sat down and took a glance.

The traveler knows not his mortal day,
Nor does he know the people who hate.
Why would he be so sad but not be gay?
 He looks at his hand and he is not in haste.

The traveler is a madman.
The ink wielder is a madman.
The traveler is a poet searching for his muse.
Hundreds of heads should call him a madman; he won't refuse.

The traveler got saw going at the front of his room.
He went back hastily and wrote beautiful lines in his book.

River of Life

In this running river called life, I did try to strive.
My body dripping with stinking sweat while trying, and I die.
Let my soul roam around in this lonely night,
Where in the presence of beautiful gazes and whispers, I will lie.

The soulful touch of different heads loving my lovely life,
I will be concerned not about their life no more.
And to this wailing, vile world, I will say goodbye.
Like a beautiful burglar, will I steal your night?

With the parting of waters maintaining their line,
I am trying, won't I continue to try?
If I am tired while trying,
And I die, bury me in this night.

Let my sorrowful soul and manly mind fight,
Let my gaudy goals and failure fight.
A man is a dead man with no lively light.

The vroom of the boat of an uplifting life
Will carry my beautiful body to a place surrounded by a lovely light.
A powerful poet's poem will be immortal, like a war god.
When his lovely lines can never be bored.

I will continue to try; why won't I try?
For I know I will be fine in this running river called life
While TRYING.
And I die, bury me in this noble night.

A Mad Man, A Sane Man

The faces of people staring at the merry mad man,
While he moves up and down—he was singing and praying fervently.
Now, who is mad?

A day

So, our skin is going to rot in the dark four-cornered pit of Mother Earth?

Death, A Gentleman?

I thought DEATH was a gentleman,
Until I passed a myriad of people.
I saw their faces swollen,
And their voices quaking, like the sound coming from speakers.
Their shouts louder than that of a destructive cacophony.

They were looking at a lifeless body on the floor.
Its skin frail and cracked,
Its eyes weeping and crawling on the floor.
Its head crushed by the gigantic leg of a massive carrier—
The end of this young and gentle soul.

The people keep weeping,
While the body keeps attracting ants and creatures of all kinds.
All my life, I thought death was a gentleman.

The Man Who Should Die And Other Poems

THE

END

www.ingramcontent.com/pod-product-compliance
Lightning Source LLC
Chambersburg PA
CBHW060839190426
43197CB00040B/2686